Table of Contents

INTRODUCTION

Cat, (Felis catus), also called house cat or domestic cat, domesticated member of the family Felidae, order Carnivora, and the smallest member of that family. Like all felids, domestic cats are characterized by supple low-slung bodies; finely molded heads, long tails that aid in balance, and specialized teeth and claws that adapt them admirably to a life of active hunting. Cats possess other features of their wild relatives in being basically carnivorous, remarkably agile and powerful, and finely coordinated in movement.

It is noteworthy that the ancestors of the other common household pet, the dog, were social animals that lived together in packs in which there was subordination to a leader, and the dog has readily transferred its allegiance from pack leader to human master. The cat, however, has not yielded as readily to subjugation. Consequently, the house cat is able to revert to complete self-reliance more quickly and more successfully than most domesticated dogs.

The "cat pattern," established very early in the evolution of modern mammals, was a successful one: early cats were already typical in form at a time when the ancestors of most other modern mammalian types were scarcely recognizable. They first appeared in the early Pliocene Epoch(5.3 to 3.6 million years ago), and they have continued with remarkably little change into modern times.

Although the origin of the domesticated cat is hidden in antiquity, studies involving mitochondrial DNA (mtDNA) suggest that there have been two lineages of Felis catus. One lineage (F. silvestris silvestris) appeared in Asia Minor possibly as early as 6,400 years ago and dispersed northward and westward into Europe. The other lineage appeared in Egypt sometime between 6,400 and 1,000 years ago before spreading throughout the Mediterranean (possibly through human introduction) along paths that paralleled the region's trade routes. Cats of both lineages continued to breed with the African wildcat (F. silvestris lybica) during their respective dispersals.

CHAPTER ONE

The cat (or domestic cat, house cat) (Felis catus) is a member of the Felidae family of the Carnivora order of the mammals. The domesticated cat has been associated with humans for at least 9,500 years, and it is one of humankind's most popular pet animals. The numerous adaptations that allow it to be an effective predator of agricultural and household pests, such as rodents, also have made it valued in human society, and likewise is prized for the companionship and wonder it brings to people.

Characteristics

Domestic cats are considered to be descended from the wild cat Felis silvestris, which is found naturally over much of Europe, Asia, and Africa, and which is one of the smaller members of the cat family. It is thought that the original ancestor of the domestic cat is the African subspecies, Felis silvestris lybca. Wild cats weigh about 3 to 8 kg (6 to 18 lbs) and domestic cats typically weigh between 2.5 and 7 kg (5.5 to 16 pounds); however, some breeds of domestic cat, such as the Maine coon, can exceed 11.3 kg (25 pounds). Some have been known to reach up to 23 kg (50 pounds) due to overfeeding. Conversely, very small cats (less than 1.8 kg / 4.0 lb) have been reported. Like all members of the Felidae family, cats are specialized for a life of hunting other animals. Cats have highly specialized teeth and a digestive tract suitable to the digestion of meat. The premolar and first molar together compose the carnassial pair on each side of the mouth, which efficiently functions to shear meat like a pair of scissors. While this is present in canines, it is highly developed in felines. The cat's tongue has sharp spines, or papillae, useful for retaining and ripping flesh from a carcass. These papillae are small backward-facing hooks that contain keratin and assist in their grooming.

Cat senses are attuned for hunting. The senses of smell, hearing, and vision of cats are superior to those of humans. Cats' eyes have a reflective layer, which greatly improves their vision in dark conditions. They can not, however, see in total darkness. To aid with navigation and sensation, cats have dozens of movable vibrissae (whiskers) over their body, especially their face. Li (2005) reports that due to a mutation in an early cat ancestor, one of two genes necessary to taste sweetness has been lost by the cat family.

Thirty-two individual muscles in the ear allow for a manner of directional hearing; the cat can move each ear independently of the other. Because of this mobility, a cat can move its body in one direction and point its ears in another direction. Most cats have straight ears pointing upward. Unlike dogs, flap-eared breeds are extremely rare. (Scottish Folds are one such exceptional genetic mutation.) When angry or frightened, a cat will lay back its ears, to accompany the growling or hissing sounds it makes. Cats will also turn their ears back when they are playing or to listen to a sound coming from behind them. The angle of a cat's ears is an important clue to their mood.

Cats also possess rather loose skin; this enables them to turn and confront a predator or another cat in a fight, even when caught in a grip. The particularly loose skin at the back of the neck is known as the "scruff" and is the area by which a mother cat grips her kittens to carry them. As a result, cats have a tendency to relax and become quiet and passive when gripped there. This tendency often extends into adulthood and can be useful when attempting to treat or move an uncooperative cat. However, since an adult cat is quite a bit heavier than a kitten, a pet cat should never be carried by the scruff, but should instead have their weight supported at the rump and hind legs, and also at the chest and front paws. Often (much like a small child) a cat will lie with its head and front paws over a person's shoulder, and its back legs and rump supported under the person's arm.

Like almost all mammals, cats possess seven cervical vertebrae. They have thirteen thoracic vertebrae (compared to twelve in humans), seven lumbar vertebrae (compared to five in humans), three sacral vertebrae like most mammals (humans have five because of their bipedal posture), and twenty-two or twenty-three caudal vertebrae (humans have three to five, fused into an internal coccyx). The extra lumbar and thoracic vertebrae account for the cat's enhanced spinal mobility and flexibility, compared to humans; the caudal vertebrae form the tail, used by the cat for counterbalance to the body during quick movements.

Cats, like dogs, are digitigrades: They walk directly on their toes, the bones of their feet making up the lower part of the visible leg. Cats are capable of walking very precisely, because like all felines they directly register; that is, they place each hind paw (almost) directly in the print of the corresponding forepaw, minimizing noise and visible tracks. This also provides sure footing for their hind paws when they navigate rough terrain.

Unlike dogs and most mammals, cats walk by moving both legs on one side and then both legs on the other. Most mammals move legs on alternate sides in sequence. Cats share this unusual gait with camels, giraffes, some horses (pacers), and a few other mammals.

Like all members of family Felidae except the cheetah, cats have retractable claws. In their normal, relaxed position, the claws are sheathed with the skin and fur around the toe pads. This keeps the claws sharp by preventing wear from contact with the ground and allows the silent stalking of prey. Cats can extend their claws voluntarily on one or more paws at will. They may extend their claws in hunting or self-defense, climbing, "kneading," or for extra traction on soft surfaces. It is also possible to make a cooperative cat extend its claws by carefully pressing both the top and bottom of the paw. The curved claws may become entangled in carpet or thick fabric, which may cause injury if the cat is unable to free itself.

Most cats have five claws on their front paws, and four or five on their rear paws. Because of an ancient mutation, however, domestic cats are prone to polydactyly, and may have six or seven toes. The fifth front claw (the dewclaw) is in a more proximal position than those of the other claws. More proximally, there is a protrusion that appears to be a sixth "finger." This special feature of the front paws, on the inside of the wrists, is the carpal pad, also found on the paws of dogs. It has no function in normal walking, but is thought to be an anti-skidding device used while jumping.

Metabolism

Cats conserve energy by sleeping more than most animals, especially as they grow older. Daily durations of sleep vary, usually 12–16 hours, with

13–14 being the average. Some cats can sleep as much as 20 hours in a 24-hour period. The term cat nap refers to the cat's ability to fall asleep (lightly) for a brief period and has entered the English lexicon—someone who nods off for a few minutes is said to be "taking a cat nap."

Due to their crepuscular nature, cats often are known to enter a period of increased activity and playfulness during the evening and early morning, dubbed the "evening crazies," "night crazies," "elevenses," or "mad half-hour" by some. The temperament of a cat can vary depending on the breed and socialization. Cats with "oriental" body types tend to be thinner and more active, while cats that have a "cobby" body type tend to be heavier and less active.

The normal body temperature of a cat is between 38 and 39°C (101 and 102.2°F). A cat is considered febrile (hyper thermic) if it has a temperature of 39.5°C (103°F) or greater, or hypothermic if less than 37.5°C (100°F). For comparison, humans have a normal temperature of approximately 36.8°C

(98.6°F). A domestic cat's normal heart rate ranges from 140 to 220 beats per minute (bpm), and is largely dependent on how excited the cat is. For a cat at rest, the average heart rate should be between 150 and 180 bpm, about twice that of a human.

Cats enjoy heat and solar exposure, often sleeping in a sunny area during the heat of the day. Cats prefer warmer temperatures than humans do. People start to feel uncomfortable when their skin's temperature gets higher than about 44.5°C (112°F), but cats do not start to show signs of discomfort until their skin reaches about 52°C (126°F).

Being closely related to desert animals, cats can easily withstand the heat and cold of a temperate climate, but not for extended periods. Although certain breeds such as the Norwegian forest cat and Maine coon have developed heavier coats of fur than other cats, they have little resistance against moist cold (eg, fog, rain, and snow) and struggle to maintain their proper body temperature when wet.

Most cats dislike immersion in water; one major exception is the Turkish Van breed, also known as the swimming cat, which originated in the Lake Van area of Turkey and has an unusual fondness for water.

Domestication and relationship with humans

In 2004, a grave was excavated in Cyprus that contained the skeletons, laid close to one another, of both a human and a cat. The grave is estimated to be 9,500 years old. This is evidence that cats have been associating with humans for a long time.

It is believed that wild cats chose to live in or near human settlements in order to hunt rodents that were feeding on crops and stored food and also to avoid other predators that avoid humans. It also is likely that wild cat kittens were sometimes found and brought home as pets. Naturalist Hans Kruuk observed people in northern Kenya doing just that. He also mentions that their domestic cats look just like the local wild cats.

Like other domesticated animals, cats live in a mutualistic arrangement with humans. It is believed that the benefit of removing rats and mice from humans' food stores outweighed the trouble of extending the protection of a human settlement to a formerly wild animal, almost certainly for humans who had adopted a farming economy. Unlike the dog, which also hunts and kills rodents, the cat does not eat grains, fruits, or vegetables. A cat that is good at hunting rodents is referred to as a mouser. In Argentina, cats are used to kill vampire bats (Kruuk 2002).

The simile "like herding cats" refers to the seeming intractability of the ordinary house cat to training in anything, unlike dogs. Despite cohabitation in colonies, cats are lone hunters. It is no coincidence that cats are also "clean" animals; the chemistry of their saliva, expended during their frequent grooming, appears to be a natural deodorant. If so, the function of this cleanliness may be to decrease the chance a prey animal will notice the cat's presence. In contrast, dog's odor is an advantage in hunting, for a dog is a pack hunter; part of the pack stations itself upwind, and its odor drives prey towards the rest of the pack stationed downwind. This requires a cooperative effort, which in turn requires communications skills. No such communications skills are required of a lone hunter. It is likely this lack of communication skills is part of the reason interacting with such an animal is problematic; cats in particular are labeled as opaque or inscrutable, if not obtuse, as well as aloof and self-sufficient. However, cats can be very affectionate towards their human companions, especially if they imprint on them at a very young age and are treated with consistent affection.

Human attitudes toward cats vary widely. Some people keep cats for companionship as pets. Others go to great lengths to pamper their cats, sometimes treating them as if they were children. When a cat bonds with its human guardian, the cat may, at times, display behaviors similar to that of a human. Such behavior may include a trip to the litter box before bedtime or snuggling up close to its companion in bed or on the sofa. Other such behavior includes mimicking sounds of the owner or using certain sounds the cat picks up from the human; sounds representing specific needs of the cat, which the owner would recognize, such as a specific tone of meow along with eye contact that may represent "I'm hungry." The cat may also be capable of learning to communicate with the human using non-spoken language or body language such as rubbing for affection (confirmation), facial expressions, and making eye contact with the owner if something needs to be addressed (e.g., finding a bug crawling on the floor for the owner to get rid of). Some owners like to train their cat to perform "tricks" commonly exhibited by dogs such as jumping, though this is rare.

Allergies to cat dander are one of the most common reasons people cite for disliking cats. However, in some instances, humans find the rewards of cat companionship outweigh the discomfort and problems associated with these allergies. Many choose to cope with cat allergies by taking prescription allergy medicine and bathing their cats frequently, since weekly bathing will eliminate about 90 percent of the cat dander present in the environment. In rural areas, farms often have dozens of semi-feral cats. Hunting in the barns and the fields, they kill and eat rodents that would otherwise spoil large parts of the grain crop. Many pet cats successfully hunt and kill rabbits, rodents, birds, lizards, frogs, fish, and large insects by instinct, but might not eat their prey. They may even present their kills, dead or maimed, to their humans, perhaps expecting them to praise or reward them, or possibly even to complete the kill and eat the mouse. Others speculate that the behavior is a part of the odd relationship between human and cat, in which the cat is sometimes a "kitten" (playing, being picked up, and carried) and sometimes an adult (teaching these very large and peculiar human kittens how to hunt by demonstrating what the point of it all is).

Behavior

Social behavior

Many people characterize cats as "solitary" animals. Cats are highly social; a primary difference in social behavior between cats and dogs (to which they are often compared) is that cats do not have a social survival strategy, or a "pack mentality;" however, this only means that cats take care of their basic needs on their own (e.g., finding food, and defending themselves). This is not the same state as being asocial. One example of how domestic cats are "naturally" meant to behave is to observe feral domestic cats, which often live in colonies, but in which each individual basically looks after itself.

The domestic cat is social enough to form colonies, but does not hunt in groups as lions do. Some breeds like Bengal, Ocicat, and Manx are known to be very social. While each cat holds a distinct territory (sexually active males having the largest territories, and neutered cats having the smallest), there are "neutral" areas where cats watch and greet one another without territorial conflicts. Outside these neutral areas, territory holders usually aggressively chase away stranger cats, at first by staring, hissing, and growling, and if that does not work, by short but noisy and violent attacks. Fighting cats make themselves appear more impressive and threatening by raising their fur and arching their backs, thus increasing their visual size. Cats also behave this way while playing. Attacks usually comprise powerful slaps to the face and body with the forepaws as well as bites, but serious damage is rare; usually the loser runs away with little more than a few scratches to the face, and perhaps the ears. Cats will also throw themselves to the ground in a defensive posture to rake with their powerful hind legs.

Normally, serious negative effects will be limited to possible infections of the scratches and bites; though these have been known to sometimes kill cats if untreated. In addition, such fighting is believed to be the primary route of transmission of feline immunodeficiency virus (FIV). Sexually active males will usually be in many fights during their lives, and often have decidedly battered faces with obvious scars and cuts to the ears and nose. Not only males will fight; females will also fight over territory or to defend their kittens, and even neutered cats will defend their (smaller) territories aggressively.

Living with humans is a symbiotic social adaptation that has developed over thousands of years. The sort of social relationship cats have with their human keepers is hard to map onto more generalized wild cat behavior, but it is certain that the cat thinks of the human differently than it does other cats (i.e., it does not think of itself as human, nor that the human is a cat). This can be seen in the difference in body and vocal language it uses with the human, when compared to how it communicates with other cats in the household, for example. Some have suggested that, psychologically, the human keeper of a cat is a sort of surrogate for the cat's mother, and that adult domestic cats live forever in a kind of suspended kitten hood.

Fondness for heights

Most breeds of cat have a noted fondness for settling in high places, or perching. Animal behaviorists have posited a number of explanations, the most common being that height gives the cat a better observation point, allowing it to survey its "territory" and become aware of activities of people and other pets in the area. In the wild, a higher place may serve as a concealed site from which to hunt; domestic cats are known to strike prey by pouncing from such a perch as a tree branch, as does a leopard .

If a cat falls, it can almost always right itself and land on its feet. This "righting reflex" is a natural instinct and is found even in newborn kittens.

This fondness for high spaces, however, can dangerously test the popular notion that a cat "always lands on its feet." The American Society for the Prevention of Cruelty to Animals warns owners to safeguard the more dangerous perches in their homes, to avoid "high-rise syndrome," where an overconfident cat falls from an extreme height. Domestic cats, especially young kittens, are known for their love of string play. Many cats cannot resist a dangling piece of string, or a piece of rope drawn randomly and enticingly across the floor. This well known love of string is often depicted in cartoons and photographs, which show kittens or cats playing with balls of yarn. It is probably related to hunting instincts, including the common practice of kittens hunting their mother's and each other's tails. If string is ingested, however, it can become caught in the cat's stomach or intestines, causing illness, or in extreme cases, death. Due to possible complications caused by ingesting a string, string play is sometimes replaced with a laser pointer's dot, which some cats will chase. Some also discourage the use of laser pointers for pet play, however, because of the potential damage to sensitive eyes and/or the possible loss of satisfaction associated with the successful capture of an actual prey object, play or real. While caution is called for, there are no documented cases of feline eye damage from a laser pointer, and the combination of precision needed and low energy involved make it a remote risk. A common compromise is to use the laser pointer to draw the cat to a prepositioned toy so the cat gets a reward at the end of the chase.

Ecology

Feeding

Cats are highly specialized for hunting, compared to members of other carnivore families such as dogs and bears. This might be related to the cats' inability to taste sugars. Since they have a greatly reduced need to digest plants, their digestive tract has evolved to be shorter, too short for effective digestion of plants but less of a weight penalty for the rapid movement required for hunting. Hunting likewise has become central to their behavior patterns, even to their predilection for short bursts of intense exercise punctuating long periods of rest. Like other members of the cat family, domestic cats are very effective predators. They ambush and immobilize vertebrate prey using tactics similar to those of leopards and tigers by pouncing; then they deliver a lethal neck bite with their long canine teeth that severs the victim's spinal cord, causes fatal bleeding by puncturing the carotid artery or the jugular vein, or asphyxiates it by crushing its trachea. The domestic cat hunts and eats over a thousand species, many of them invertebrates, especially insects.

Even well-fed domestic cats may hunt and kill birds, mice, rats, scorpions, cockroaches, grasshoppers, and other small animals in their environment. They often present such trophies to their owner. The motivation is not entirely clear, but friendly bonding behaviors are often associated with such an action. Ethologist Paul Leyhausen, in an extensive study of social and predatory behavior in domestic cats (documented in his book Cat Behavior), proposed a mechanism to explain this presenting behavior. In simple terms, cats adopt humans into their social group, and share excess kill with others in the group according to the local pecking order, in which humans place at or near the top. Another possibility is that presenting the kill might be a relic of a kitten feline behavior of demonstrating, for its mother's approval, that it has developed the necessary skill for hunting.

Reproduction

Female cats can come into heat several times a year. Males are attracted by the scent of the female's urine and by her calls and may fight with each other for the right to mate.

The gestation period for cats is approximately 63–65 days. The size of a litter averages three to five kittens, with the first litter usually smaller than subsequent litters. As in most carnivore young, newborn kittens are very small, blind, and helpless. They are cared for by their mother in a hidden nest or den that she prepares. Kittens are weaned at between six and seven weeks, and cats normally reach sexual maturity at 4–10 months (females) and to 5–7 months (males).

Nomenclature

A group of cats is referred to as a clowder. A male cat is called a tom (or a gib, if neutered), and a female is called a queen. The male progenitor of a cat, especially a pedigreed cat, is its sire, and its female progenitor is its dam. An immature cat is called a kitten (which is also an alternative name for young rats, rabbits, hedgehogs, beavers, squirrels, and skunks). In medieval Britain, the word kitten was interchangeable with the word catling.

A cat whose ancestry is formally registered is called a pedigreed cat, purebred cat, or a show cat (although not all show cats are pedigreed or purebred). In strict terms, a purebred cat is one whose ancestry contains only individuals of the same breed. A pedigreed cat is one whose ancestry is recorded, but may have ancestors of different breeds (almost exclusively new breeds; cat registries are very strict about which breeds can be mated together). Cats of unrecorded mixed ancestry are referred to as domestic longhairs and domestic shorthairs or commonly as random-bred, moggies, mongrels, mutt-cats, or alley cats. The ratio of pedigree/purebred cats to random-bred cats varies from country to country. However, generally speaking, purebreds are less than ten percent of the total feline population.

The word "cat" derives from Old English catt, which belongs to a group of related words in European languages, including Welsh cath, Spanish gato, Basque katu, Byzantine Greek κάττα, Old Irish cat, German Katze, and Old Church Slavonic kotka. The ultimate source of all these terms is unknown, although it may be linked to the ancient Nubian kadis and the Berber kadiska. The term puss (as in pussycat) may come from Dutch (from poes, a female cat, or the diminutive poesje, an endearing term for any cat) or from other Germanic languages.

History of cats and humans

Egypt

After associating with humans for several thousand years, cats entered the historical record in ancient Egypt. The first known painting of a cat dates to about 3,000 B.C.E.

Cats became very important in Egyptian society. They were associated with Bast, the goddess of the home, the domestic cat, protector of the fields and home from vermin infestations, and who sometimes took on the warlike aspect of a lioness. The first domesticated cats may have saved early Egyptians from many rodent infestations and likewise, Bast developed from the adoration for her feline companions. She was the daughter of the sun god Ra and played a significant role in Egyptian religion.

Cats were protected in Egypt and when they died their bodies were mummified. Some historians report that killing a cat was punishable by death and that when a family cat died family members would shave their eyebrows in mourning.

Roman and Medieval times

The Egyptians tried to prevent the export of cats from their country, but after Rome conquered Egypt in 30 B.C.E., pet cats became popular in Rome and were introduced throughout the Roman Empire. Judaism considered the cat an unclean animal and cats are not mentioned in the Bible. As Christianity came to dominate European society, cats began to be looked on less favorably, often being thought to be associated with witchcraft. On some feast days, they were tortured and killed as a symbolic way of driving out the devil.

Islam, however, looked at cats more favorably. It is said by some writers that Muhammad had a favorite cat, Muezza. It is said he loved cats so much that "he would do without his cloak rather than disturb one that was sleeping on it".

During this time, pet cats also became popular over much of Asia. In different locations, distinct breeds of cats arose because of different environments and because of selection by humans. It is possible that interbreeding with local wild cats might have also played a part in this. Among the Asian cat breeds that developed this way are: The Persian, the Turkish Angora, the Siberian, and the Siamese. In Japan, the Maneki Neko is a small figurine of a cat that is thought to bring good fortune.

Modern times

In the Renaissance, Persian cats were brought to Italy and Turkish Angora cats were brought to France and then to England. Interest in different breeds of cats developed, especially among the wealthy. In 1871, the first cat exhibition was held in the Crystal Palace in London. Pet cats have continued to grow in popularity. It is estimated that 31 percent of United States households own at least one cat and the total number of pet cats in the United States is over 70 million.

Cats have also become very popular as subjects for paintings and as characters in children's books and cartoons.

Domesticated varieties

The list of cat breeds is quite large: Most cat registries recognize between 30 and 40 breeds of cats, and several more are in development, with one or more new breeds being recognized each year on average, having distinct features and heritage. The owners and breeders of show cats compete to see whose animal bears the closest resemblance to the "ideal" definition of the breed. Because of common crossbreeding in populated areas, many cats are simply identified as belonging to the homogeneous breeds of domestic longhair and domestic shorthair, depending on their type of fur.

Feral cats

Feral cats, domestic cats that have returned to the wild, are common throughout the world. In some places, especially islands that have no natural carnivores, they have been very destructive to native species of birds and other small animals. The Invasive Species Specialist Group has put the cat on its list of the "World's 100 Worst Invasive Species". The impacts of feral cats greatly depends on country or landmass. In the northern hemisphere, most landmasses have fauna adapted to wildcat species and other placental mammal predators. Here it may be argued that the potential for feral cats to cause damage is little unless cat numbers are very high, or the region supports unusually vulnerable native wildlife species. A notable exception is Hawaii, where feral cats have had extremely serious impacts on native birds species; "naive" fauna on islands of all sizes, in both hemispheres, are particularly vulnerable to feral cats.

In the southern hemisphere, there are many landmasses, including Australia, where cat species did not occur historically, and other placental mammal predators were rare or absent. Native species there are ecologically vulnerable and behaviorally "naive" to predation by feral cats. Feral cats have had extremely serious impacts on these wildlife species and have played a leading role in the endangerment and extinction of many of them. It is clear that in Australia, a large quantity of native birds, lizards, and small marsupials are taken every year by feral cats, and feral cats have played a role in driving some small marsupial species to extinction. Some organizations in Australia are now creating fenced islands of habitat for endangered species that are free of feral cats and foxes.

Feral cats may live alone, but most are found in large groups called feral colonies with communal nurseries, depending on resource availability. Some lost or abandoned pet cats succeed in joining these colonies, although animal welfare organizations note that few are able to survive long enough to become feral, most being killed by vehicles, or succumbing to starvation, predators, exposure, or disease. Most abandoned cats probably have little alternative to joining a feral colony. The average lifespan of such feral cats is much shorter than a domestic housecat, which can live sixteen years or more. Urban areas in the developed world are not friendly, nor adapted environments for cats; most domestic cats are descended from cats in desert climates and were distributed throughout the world by humans. Nevertheless, some feral cat colonies are found in large cities such as around the Colosseum and Forum Romanum in Rome.

Although cats are adaptable, feral felines are unable to thrive in extreme cold and heat, and with a very high protein requirement, few find adequate nutrition on their own in cities. They have little protection or understanding of the dangers from dogs, coyotes, and even automobiles. However, there are thousands of volunteers and organizations that trap these unadoptable feral felines, spay or neuter them, immunize the cats against rabies and feline leukemia, and treat them with long-lasting flea products. Before releasing them back into their feral colonies, the attending veterinarian often nips the tip off one ear to mark the feral as spayed/neutered and inoculated, since these cats will more than likely find themselves trapped again.

Volunteers continue to feed and give care to these cats throughout their lives, and not only is their lifespan greatly increased, but behavior and nuisance problems, due to competition for food, are also greatly reduced. In time, if an entire colony is successfully spayed and neutered, no additional kittens are born and the feral colony disappears. Many hope to see an end to urban feral cat colonies through these efforts.

Special traits

The cat has a subtle repertoire of facial expressions, vocal sounds, and tail and body postures that express its emotional state and intentions. These various signals serve to increase, decrease, or maintain social distance. One distinctive social behavior involves rubbing the side of the head, lips, chin, or tail against the owner and against furniture. These regions of the cat's body contain scent glands that seem to play a role in establishing a familiar odor in the cat's environment.

The tongue of all cats, which has a patch of sharp, backward-directed spines called filiform papillae near the tip, has the appearance and feel of a coarse file; the spines help the cat to groom itself. The disposition to cleanliness is well established in cats, and they groom themselves at length, especially after meals.

While lions and other big cats roar, domestic cats and other Felis species purr. Purring has been described as a low, continuous, rattling hum and often is interpreted as an expression of pleasure or contentment. Purring also occurs in cats that are injured and in pain, however, so that this vocalization can be seen as the cat's "mantra"—that is, as a relaxing, self-comforting sound and a friendly mood-conveying signal.

Behavioral problems

Under conditions of domestication, the cat is subject to a variety of factors that result in behavior indicative of emotional distress and difficulty in adapting to the home environment. Some behaviors are not abnormal but are difficult for owners to accept.

The most common behavior problem in companion cats is that they sometimes urinate and defecate outside the litter box in the house. Organic causes include feline urologic syndrome (urinary bladder inflammation and calculi, or stones, in the urinary tract), blocked or impacted anal glands, and constipation. Emotional causes include the addition of a new family member—another cat, a child, or a spouse. Such changes may make the cat feel insecure, so that it deposits urine and feces around the house, possibly as territorial marks for security. Cats are creatures of habit, and any change in the family structure or in daily routines—resulting, for example, from a move or even from rearranging furniture—can be stressful.

Another common behavior problem in cats is their natural desire to rake objects such as drapes and furniture with their claws. Surgical removal of the front claws to prevent property damage is normally repugnant to cat lovers. Cats can be trained to use carpeted scratching posts in the house to satisfy this behavioral need, which may be a combination of claw cleaning and sharpening and of territorial marking.

Many cats engage in social licking and in the grooming of their feline and human companions, which is a natural display of affection and dependence. Some also engage in nursing behavior, sucking on people's fingers and earlobes, on their own paws and tails, and on blankets and woolen clothing. Nursing may be a cat's way of regressing and relaxing into kittenish behavior. It is often more intense in cats weaned too early or in those malnourished in kitten hood. For various emotional reasons some cats may groom themselves to the point of self-mutilation or become compulsive wool suckers and eaters.

Pica—a hunger for nonnutritive substances—may be a symptom of the need for more roughage in the diet or of feline leukemia or other health problems. As with the dog, excessive eating and drinking is frequently associated with endocrine diseases such as diabetes and thyroiddy's function. Cats often vomit soon after eating, which is most often caused by the accumulation of fur balls in the stomach, although a food allergy, feline leukemia, or other organic cause may be involved.

Active and healthy cats often race through the house as though they were crazed. These "evening crazies" (which can also erupt early in the morning) result from the cat's ancient rhythm of actively hunting around dawn and dusk. In the domestic environment, this normal, instinctive behavior often still occurs, to the consternation of some owners who fear that their cat may have rabies, a brain tumor, or an unstable personality.

Changes in animals' behavior should not, therefore, be dismissed as psychological (or as simple disobedience, as when a cat suddenly becomes housebroken, for example), since there may be an underlying physical cause. Nevertheless, abnormal behavior in animals often does have a nonphysical, psychological, or emotional origin, which should always be considered in the diagnosis and treatment of the ailments of companion animals.

Other traits

The cat's sleep patterns are different from those of dogs and humans. Dogs and humans have long periods of REM (rapid eye movement) sleep, the stage that is associated with dreaming. In contrast, the cat rarely lapses into REM sleep. Instead, it has a lighter, episodic sleep pattern that enables it to rest but to be instantly alert. When sick, cats have a tendency to withdraw and become inactive, which helps them conserve energy. A sick cat may seem lifeless but recover after a few days of withdrawal, which is one reason cats are said to have nine lives. (A sick cat should always be taken to a veterinarian, however; it is negligent simply to let nature take its course.)

Cats are known to have traveled hundreds of miles to find their owners in new homes to which they themselves have never been. Dogs have also performed such feats of so-called psi (psychic) trailing. Scientists have not been able to find a physiological or psychological explanation for this ability.

Cats As Pets

The popularity of the cat, especially of pedigreed breeds, has continued to grow. The cat's independent personality, grace, cleanliness, and subtle displays of affection have wide appeal. Typically, cats are creatures of habit; they are inquisitive, but not adventurous, and are easily upset by sudden changes of routine. The ideal household cat has been separated from its mother between the ages of two and four months, raised in a clean home, kept away from unhealthy animals, and inoculated against common infectious cat diseases. Although cats often enjoy the company of other cats, especially when raised together from kittenhood, introducing a strange cat to other cats in the home can cause stress, aggression, and other behaviour problems. Cats are generally less sociable than dogs, who more readily accept a new pack member.

A good disposition and good health are important criteria for choosing a cat. Disposition varies only slightly between male and female cats. There are, however, distinct differences in disposition among the various pedigreed varieties; the Siamese, for example, is vocal and demanding, while the Persian is quiet and fastidious. The mixed breed, or "alley cat," is a heterogeneous breed of unknown lineage; therefore, its disposition is difficult to assess. By chance, the mixed breed may prove a happier and healthier pet than a pedigreed one. On the other hand, the behaviour and vigour of the direct ancestors of pedigreed cats are indicative of the characteristics the offspring will possess as adults. But, as with the propagation of purebred dogs, the proliferation of pedigreed cats has resulted in an increase in inherited diseases, a major reason many people prefer mongrels or mixed breeds.

CHAPTER TWO

How to Train a Kitten

Cats are not small dogs, and as a result training a cat isn't exactly the same as training a dog. Generally speaking, the process of training a cat is more challenging for people accustomed to training dogs or other animals because kittens are much more independent and less interested in the opinions of humans than other house pets. However, with the proper techniques and lots of patience, you can train your kitten to be a happy, healthy, and mostly obedient companion.

Socializing Your Kitten

Let the kitten's mother socialize it for at least eight weeks.

Generally, a kitten needs at least two months of socialization with its mother before they can be separated. During this time, the mother should do most of the "training" we associate with having a good, well-behaved house cat.

• Kittens start weaning at around a month and will be fully weaned and should be eating solid food by eight weeks.

• If your cat has had a litter of kittens and you're weaning them yourself, it's absolutely essential that you let it take at least two months before you separate them completely. The mother should train the kitten to know its strength, eat properly, and use the litter box.

•

Avoid buying kittens who have been weaned too early.

If you're buying a kitten from the store, make sure you discover exactly how old it is. Kittens who are weaned too early tend to be more aggressive and will require more training than properly weaned kittens.

Continue to socialize your kitten.

The best pets are those which are properly socialized at a young age. A well socialized kitten should be handled from 2 weeks of age, by a variety of people - young and old, and of different genders and physical appearances. This handling should take place every day, ideally for 5 - 10 minutes at least twice a day - the more often the better.

• If your kitten is not socialized and used to people, you will face an uphill struggle to train the kitten. This is because the kitten will be wary of people and not not trust them. Thus your first task is to win the kitten's confidence.

• If the kitten is already older than 8 weeks and not used to people, they are likely to behave like a feral or "wild" kitten. Unfortunately, once this behavior is established it is difficult to break and the likelihood is the kitten will grow into an anti social cat.

Be patient when socializing your kitten.

You cannot force a kitten or cat to do anything, and so your weapons are patience and providing positive rewards when the kitten is around so they begin to link you to nice experiences.

• Examples of this include lying on the floor when you watch TV, and keeping a treat or two in your hand or pocket. By lying down you pose less of a threat and so a curious kitten may advance toward you. By dropping a treat on the floor this rewards the kitten's boldness and may help them to link people to tasty snacks, and make them more willing to approach in future.

Use positive reinforcement.

Rubbing a cat's face in messes that it makes, or yelling loudly, is a terrible way to train kittens. Positive reinforcement is accomplished by rewarding behavior that you want the cat to repeat, so that the cat will eventually abandon the old behaviors that you want the cat to avoid. This is the easiest way to change a cat's behavior.

• If a cat does something you don't like, ignore the cat. Usually, whining at the door or clawing at something is a way of getting your attention. If it doesn't work, the cat will soon abandon the behavior entirely.

• A reward might be a tasty treat. Most cats have one "must have" treat. If your kitten doesn't seem food motivated, then try them with a variety of foods to see which one excites them.

Avoid punishing the kitten.

Punishing the kitten may make a superficial improvement but the cat will merely become more devious. Take the scenario where the cat urinates in the middle of the lounge room carpet. If you punish or frighten the kitten, they will link the punishment to you rather than urinating on the carpet. Thus, the kitten will become careful not to urinate in front of you in the future.

• This can also backfire because the kitten is more likely to seek hidey-holes to urinate, or alternatively, become hesitant to use the litter tray when you are about because they are wary of you.

Make the sounds the mother cat makes when you disapprove of a kitten's behavior.

When mother cats chastise kittens, they make a kind of clicking sound at the back of the throat that is possible to mimic. It's much more effective and in-line with the training of kitten to attempt to do basically what the kitten is used to.

• All you've got to do is click your tongue against the roof of your mouth when the kitten is clawing something or doing something that's against the rules of the house.

Use catnip to help with training.

Training a cat with catnip can be extremely effective and rewarding your kitten with treats will work better than yelling. This can be a great way of attracting cats toward scratching posts, toys you want them to play with, or getting them to sleep in particular areas that you want them to sleep in. A bit of catnip placed in a bag can keep a cat entertained for hours.

• Not all cats are attracted to catnip, making your job somewhat more difficult. If your cat doesn't seem interested, you can try using something the cat does like, like a little treat of food, to attract it toward something.

Provide lots of cat spaces.

If your kitten keeps climbing up on the kitchen counter to observe the scene or getting into areas it shouldn't, scaring the cat off won't' work. This only teaches cats that they should fear you. Instead, put a platform or a bench in an adjacent area, or put some catnip or some treats on it, so the cat can jump up and watch the entire area from above.

• Make it clear that this is the cat's zone. If the cat jumps on the counter again, move them to the bench.

Play with the kitten regularly.

To keep kittens from acting out, integrate exercise into the cat's feeding routine. Before every meal, set off their hunting instincts by playing with some string, ribbon, a laser pointer, or some other toy the cat enjoys. This is an essential part of cats' daily routine. Without it they can get moody or over excited.

• Get out a toy and have the cat jumping up in the air running around, then let the cat catch it then proceed to dinner. Typically, cats will then groom and sleep after meals. Play for at least 20 minutes a day, or until kitty stops.

Training Kittens to Eat

Figure out if you can simply leave food out for your kitten at all times.

There are two basic philosophies when it comes to feeding cats, and it will largely depend on how your cat eats. Generally, you can take a constant feeding or a timed feeding approach for most cats, but not both. Some cats are fine with a full bowl of food left out at all times, from which they will eat until they're not hungry anymore. This is probably the easiest for you, as long as your cat can control their intake properly.

• When food is available all the time, this is known as ad lib feeding. This mimics how a cat eats in the wild, which is to take frequent small snacks. A cat that is not bored and has plenty to entertain them and provide mental stimulation, is usually fine at controlling their calorie intake and can be trusted with ad lib feeding.

Feed the kitten at regular times if it tends to overeat. The problems tend to arise if the cat is bored, or under stimulated, in which case eating can become a hobby and the cat loses control of their calorie intake.

• Often, these are the cats who will whine for food when it isn't present, as well, making it important that you start feeding on a regular schedule. Kittens should usually be fed four times a day until they are 12 weeks old, and then 3 times a day until they are 6 months old. After this an adult cat can be fed twice daily, in the morning and at night. Do it at the same time each day.

Feed the kitten the proper food.

Kittens will often double or triple their weight in the first few weeks of growth, meaning that kittens will usually need to eat a diet higher in calories and fat than adult cats will. Commercial food is generally separated by the age of the cat who'll be eating it, and it's usually the best idea to feed a kitten food.

• Don't feed a kitten food for adult or geriatric cats, and don't feed an adult or geriatric cat kitten food. The calories in these types of food are drastically different and can lead to either malnutrition, in the case of the kitten eating adult food, or excess weight, in the case of the adult cat eating kitten food.

Provide clean water for the cat at all times.

Cats will start whining if they don't have something that they need, and this whining can turn into a long-term habit that can be quite annoying. If you don't want to have to re-train a kitten, make sure you do it right in the first place. If a cat knows that it's water bowl will be refilled before it gets empty, it'll never occur to the kitten to start whining for you to refill it. Stay on top of all your cat chores.

Do not feed the cat from the table.

Aside from the fact that kittens shouldn't eat many common human foods, like garlic, onions, chocolate, grapes, and raisins, which are toxic to cats, feeding a cat from the table will have your kitten clambering around every time you're trying to eat food. Only feed your kitten cat food, and feed it at appropriate times.

• Never give a cat milk. Despite the common misconception that cats should be fed saucers of milk, dairy is indigestible to cats, and will result in an extremely disgusting litter box for you to clean up the next day.

• Cats should only eat tuna as an occasional treat say once or twice a week. While many cats love this canned fish, it doesn't contain the nutritional elements that cats need for all-around health, and it's increasingly common that some cats can become overly addicted to eating tuna, at the expense of other more nutritious foods. It'd be like a human eating nothing but potato chips.

Training Your Kitten to Use the Litter Box

Get a simple litter box.

The simplest litter boxes are usually the most friendly to the cat. A simple tray full of fresh, clean litter is the most inviting environment for the cat to do its business. If you've got a complicated automated litter box, it can be frightening or intimidating to use.

• Likewise, litter boxes with lids on top can help to keep the mess contained, but it can also make it more difficult for the cat to access the litter box. If you're struggling to get your cat in the box, try using a simpler, uncovered litter box.

• If you don't want to scoop cat poop, don't get a cat. There are all kinds of complicated contraptions and products designed to make it less messy, but the fact of the matter is that cleaning up after a cat is something you're going to have to do to keep the cat happy.

Place the kitten in the litter box.

If you want your cat to use the litter box, usually all you'll have to do is place them in it. Cats want to do their business in litter boxes, so it shouldn't be any more difficult than literally placing them inside of it once to show them where it is.

• Some trainers recommend sitting with your cat and physically forcing them to paw the litter a few times, to get used to the feeling and to familiarize themselves with the environment. The idea is to trigger the instinctive reaction of a cat to scrape and cover up their feces after using the tray.

• If the kitten becomes distressed by you holding their paws to make the scraping motion, then just abandon the idea.

Place the litter tray in a quiet place, ideally in the corner of a room.

This is a good location because the kitten feels vulnerable when going to the bathroom. By having a wall on either side, the cat only has to watch for predators approaching from the front.

• Also, avoid putting the litter tray next to a washing machine or any device that makes a sudden noise or movement. If the machine goes into spin cycle while the kitten is on the tray, and the kitten gets a fright, it will discourage him or her from using the tray in the future.

Clean the litter box regularly.

Cats, even kittens, want to use the litter box and it shouldn't be difficult to get them to go inside it. The primary reason that cats begin to urinate or defecate outside of their litter box is that they find the litter box environment unusable. This is either because the litter box is too difficult to get to, you've changed litter too regularly, or the litter box is too messy.

• Litter boxes need to be cleaned every single day. Use a scoop to remove the feces and the urine clumps, and change the litter regularly to keep it fresh. If the litter box smells bad to you, it smells terrible to your cat. Keep that in mind.

Use one kind of litter on a regular basis.

Changing the type of cat litter you use can be confusing for the cat. Ideally, you need to use unscented and natural pine-based cat litters to provide the best environment.

• Avoid using scented cat litter. These may smell nice to us but the scent is overpowering to a kitten, who has a much more sensitive nose. This may deter them from using the box.

• Use enough fresh litter in the litter box so that the cat has enough room to paw around. Cats don't want to paw around in their own urine any more than you would want to.

Avoid putting anything but litter in the litter box.

Don't try to entice cats to use the litter box by putting toys, treats, or food into the litter. Cats don't want to eat where they defecate, and putting food in the litter box will make it much more confusing for your cat to know where to do their business.

Training Your Kitten With a Clicker

Introduce clicker training when your cat is a kitten. That is an ideal time to introduce clicker training. A clicker makes a click-clack noise that you use to mark the exact moment of the behavior you wish the cat to repeat. This is a great way of teaching a cat to do tricks, or even useful things like coming to you when called.

Associate the clicker with a treat.

Start by simply clicking and then giving your kitten a treat. When you make the click-clack noise and then give the kitten a treat, they will make a link between click-clack and a reward. Once the kitten is starting to come towards you in anticipation of the treat, press the clicker, and then give the reward. Keep repeating this until you are positive they have learned to associate the clicker with the reward.

• A food reward is ideal, but some cats are not hugely motivated by food. However, every cat has at least one food they go mad for, if you can just find out what that food is.

• Experiment with different foods including ham, tuna, chicken, fish, steak, and prawns. You'll know when you've found their favorite because it will disappear in seconds and the kitten will meow looking for more.

Train at a time when the kitten's tummy is not full, since a full stomach will take the shine off a food reward.

To start with, offer the treat to the kitten, and when they take it, at that precise moment press the clicker. Do this 3 or 4 times, then leave it at that until the next session. Repeat.

Mark the behavior you want with the click-clack of the clicker.

Once the kitten associates a clicker noise with a treat, you can adjust your clicking, which acts as a down payment on a reward, to only happen when the kitten does something good.

Connect the good-behavior clicking with a treat once the behavior is completed.

You can even team that behavior with a word such as "Sit", to complete the training.

Training Your Kitten to Come on Command

Commit to training your kitten to come when called, even though it may take some time and effort.

It can be a great thing to teach a kitten is to come when called. This is immensely useful, and can help you find your kitten if they get lost.

• Many times, a kitten that gets lost is very frightened, and instinctively the kitten goes to ground and hides as a protective mechanism. However, if they are trained to come on command, this training may overcome their nature inclination to stay put in a frightening situation.

Use short but often training sessions.

When training a kitten you need to commit to the concept of little but often training. Cats have shorter concentration spans than dogs and most likely their attention starts to wander after 5 minutes or so. A great schedule would be three, 5 minute sessions a day, or alternatively, frequent short ad hoc sessions when the kitten was around and in playful mood.

Pick a cue word to use to call the kitten.

As the kitten comes towards you, you will give the word cue you have decided to use to summon the cat. Choose a word the cat won't hear in any other context, so an unusual or even a made up word is ideal.

• It is best NOT to use the kitten's name as this will be used in other circumstances. This will confuse the cat because if they aren't expected to come when you say, "Kitty's a pretty girl", it dilutes the cue word.

Use clicker training to train the kitten to come on command.

Call the cue word and the moment the kitten turns towards you, click, to mark the moment of the desired action. Then immediately give the kitten a treat. If you repeat this regularly, over many training sessions, the cat will learn to come to that word.

• You can use this principle to train a cat to do any number of desired behaviors such as jumping down off a work surface, to shaking paws.

Training Your Kitten About Appropriate Scratching

Provide a space for the kitten to scratch.

If you're worried about your kitten scratching up your clothes or furniture, you need to provide other places for the cat to scratch. Generally, catnip-spiked scratching posts or cardboard liners with catnip underneath make the best scratching spaces for cats.

• Cats need to use their claws to keep them trimmed and healthy, meaning that they're going to need to scratch something. There's little point in punishing a cat for scratching, because they're not doing it maliciously. Cats scratch because they must.

Reward the cat when they use the scratching post. If you see the cat sharpening their claws on the post, give the cat a treat so they'll return to it.

Keep a spray bottle hand. A good way to keep cats from scratching things you don't want scratched up is to keep a water spray bottle on hand and gently spray the cat any time they scratch the object. This will have the effect of getting them away from the area immediately. After you spray the cat, hide the spray bottle. If the cat knows it was you, the cat may get fearful of you.

Use mint oil on areas you don't want the cat to scratch. Applying a small amount of essential oil, typically mint, on the area that you want the cats to avoid deters them from scratching there. This is an excellent way of keeping young kittens off any types of surfaces you'd prefer they not invade.

• The scent is a natural cat repeller. They simply don't like the smell. It's essentially harmless to the cat, just an unpleasant odor.

• Be sure to be careful applying essential oils onto surfaces that might be damaged by it. Apply on a test spot that is hidden before applying the oil to a visible surface.

CONCLUSION

If you're lucky, your cat will be willing and eager to learn your commands. However, there's a chance she'll ignore you. Every cat is different, and training can be extremely trying on your patience. Make sure to carve out small amounts of time each day to spend working with her. If you have other cats in your home, remember that they each have different personalities and have to be taught differently.

Be aware that cats do not understand or respond well to punishment. Punishment will often cause your cat to run away and hide from you, and can lead to stress, which can also breed behavioral and health problems. Encouraging good behavior with a reward is much more effective, and that reward can come in the form of praise and/or a tasty treat. This reward-based training teaches your cat to associate good behavior with positive results.

One of the most common cat training techniques is clicker training, which is another form of reward-based training. For instance, if you'd like to teach your cat to sit, click the clicker as soon as she sits down and give her a small treat. Eventually, with enough repetition, she will learn to associate the click with the behavior and the reward.

Keep training sessions short—cats have short attention spans and can get bored fast. Focus on one command at a time and move on to the next when she's mastered the first. Practice the commands in different areas of the house so that she gets used to responding to you in different situations.

Always remember to praise your cat for good behaviors as well. Give her a treat for a job well done, and she will learn to associate her actions with her rewards.

Made in the USA
Monee, IL
13 October 2022

15794124R00046